I0006519

A Multi-Modal Approach to Address

ADHD
A Non-Drug Emphasis

To Slow Down and Listen,
"Ya Gotta Have More Than Meds"

Annie M. Wells, Ph.D.
Alabama A&M University

authorHOUSE®

AuthorHouse™
1663 Liberty Drive
Bloomington, IN 47403
www.authorhouse.com
Phone: 1-800-839-8640

© 2010 Annie M. Wells, Ph.D. All rights reserved.

No part of this book may be reproduced, stored in a retrieval system, or transmitted by any means without the written permission of the author.

First published by AuthorHouse 4/13/2010

ISBN: 978-1-4490-6621-5 (sc)

Printed in the United States of America
Bloomington, Indiana

This book is printed on acid-free paper.

Foreword

This book has shed a new light on ADHD for me. As an educator and a parent of a child with ADHD, this book has defined and explained many of the questions I had about ADHD. It is not a book that is written in medical terms; it is practical, easy to understand and offers great strategies for helping not only children, but adults with ADHD as well. This book would be extremely helpful for teachers who are struggling to meet the needs of students with ADHD. The book reveals how individuals with ADHD view common day-to-day activities such as on the job and at school. Reading it allows one to better understand how ADHD may impact an individual. Again, the best thing about the book is it offers strategies and alternatives other than medication for assisting individuals with ADHD. In addition to the useful information on ADHD, the author has impeccable skills and knowledge in this area that she brings into the book. The real-life examples provided offer a clear view of the challenges posed by individuals with ADHD, their parents, teachers and other family members. I am pleased and honored to have been asked to write a foreword for this book. The author should be congratulated for providing this valuable reference book for one of the most common diagnoses of school age children today. So, if you are looking for a book on ADHD that is practical and easily understood, look no further.

Angela R. Williams, Ed.D.
Assistant Professor of Education

Acknowledgements

It is a pleasure to have colleagues, friends, and relatives to assist me in getting this book ready. First, I would like to thank my colleague, Dr. Angela Williams in the School of Education, who so graciously agreed to write the foreword to this book. She went beyond the call of duty and proofread the document and made other helpful suggestions. Most of all, she made me feel awfully good by stating many positive things about the book and me as author. Secondly, I would like to acknowledge my friend, Evelyn Wilson, who has worked in the field of education for over 25 years. I appreciate her intelligent comments, corrections, suggestions and point of view. These two friends indicated that they have had first-hand experience as a parent of a child with Attention Deficit Hyperactivity. Last, but not least, my utmost thanks to Dr. Joan Kerr, a fellow licensed practicing psychologist, for her willingness to review and provide input on this document despite a recent loss.

Dedication

This book is dedicated to the loves of my life, Mrs. Rosanna Bullard, my 91-year-old mother, and my deceased father, Robert Bullard; and Marcus L. Wells, MD, MPH and Micah D. Wells, JD, my sons. They are/have been the biggest supporters than any individual could ever have. I am so blessed to have them.

A Special Dedication

On the eve of writing this book on August 1, 2009, a giant in the area of Learning Style, Rita Dunn, passed away. She was a leader in working with children with a non-drug approach and believed that all children could learn best and up to their potential if taught the way they learn best. Rita (and her husband Ken) introduced me to learning style in 1992; soon thereafter, came the establishment of the Alabama Learning Style Center (an International Affiliate) at Alabama A&M University. The theory, research, instrumentation and the application of learning style provide the basis for Chapter 5 (the Handbook) in this document. I pause, also, to dedicate this book to Rita Dunn, a scholar, mentor and long-term friend.

About the Book

The book is organized in two main parts: general information and basic research about Attention Deficit Hyperactivity Disorders; and practical information full of psychological/behavioral and educational/learning style strategies and tips. The first part of the book provides the reader with adequate information to understand the rationale for using the techniques in the latter part. Chapters I through III provide that general and basic information, including the medical approach. Chapter I describe what the ADHD disorders are, etiological theories, DSM-IV-TR criteria, and how one makes a differential diagnosis. Chapter II acquaints parents and professionals with symptoms as early as infancy and preschool age, and what they can do when ADHD is suspected. Medical treatment is usually recommended; therefore, Chapter III deals with the medical approach and the various categories of medicines that can be used to treat the different types of ADHD. Chapters IV through V focus on the non-medical approaches. Chapter IV describes psychological/behavioral approaches to address problems of executive functions, attention, hyperactivity, impulsivity; social skills, memory and organization of time and materials. This chapter emphasizes the importance of addressing executive functions first and foremost as well as early in development to be most effective. Chapter V makes the point that learning style approaches emphasize strengths of children with ADHD rather than weaknesses; and that these children learn different. One could perceives this chapter as a handbook to use in determining which of the elements of style a child exhibits and preceding with the appropriate technique. Chapters IV and V also make the point that the non-drug approaches can yield a relatively permanent change in behavior which will take practice.

TABLE OF CONTENTS

Attention Deficit Hyperactivity Disorder (ADHD) is found worldwide.

Annie M. Wells, Ph.D.

www.avianocenter.com

Introduction

A book written about Attention Deficit Hyperactivity has worldwide implications mainly because the disorder is found on all continents. The overall prevalence in the world is 5.2 percent (Moffitt & Melchior, 2007; Polanczyk & Rohde, 2007). These authors report the rates as follows: North America 6.2%; Europe, 4.6%; Africa, 8.5%; and South America, 11.8%. Western culture does not have the monopoly of this disorder.

The purposes of this book are to focus primarily on non-medical models and approaches used to treat and educate persons with Attention Deficit Hyperactivity Disorders (ADHD); and to provide simple and practical strategies for parents, teachers, and mental health professionals. The book is interspersed with citations of research to support simple, easy suggestions for addressing the disorders. One must realize that even though there is a genetic tendency for ADHD, one may not experience severe symptoms. Similar to any condition, the phenotypic expression of the disorder may not occur if the environmental conditions are optimal. For example, if hypertension runs in the family, hypertension may not be expressed if one engages in regular exercise, eats healthy foods, and knows how to reduce and manage stressors of life.

Likewise, "for some children with mild to moderate symptoms (of ADHD) psychological intervention may prove sufficient to improve or alleviate symptoms" (Myers, 2007). However, the Guidelines of the American Academy of Pediatrics (2001) state that a care plans for children should include both psychological and medical treatment. Other Guidelines suggest that both approaches of treatment are more effective than either one approach alone. Rationale for the book stems from the fact psychological and psychoeducational intervention models of ADHD are not given equal application as the medical or disease and the deficit models.

Psychological interventions are often minimally addressed or left out of treatment entirely (Meyer,

2007). Human beings are biopsychosocial organisms; therefore, a holistic assessment, and comprehensive and multidisciplinary interventions must be considered for effectiveness. Attention Deficit Hyperactivity Disorders are more complex and require more effort than most people realize; therefore, the assessments and interventions require careful consideration. A multi-modal, multidisciplinary approach using evidence-based research must be considered seriously. Early and appropriate intervention coupled with time, work, and adherence, will yield positive changes.

An inordinate amount of controversy is written and debated about ADHD—its veracity, causes, prevalence, comorbidity, differential diagnosis, medications and other orally-ingested substances, and non-medical approaches. Writings by experts in the field indicate that there is help for persons with ADHD in the form of a variety of medications, behavior-changing therapies, and educational options. Much research is in the literature but there is a need for individuals who work with children with ADHD to study the disorder . According to O'Reily (2007) review of related literature, there may be a disinterest in the material studied, a lack of time to perform the work on behavior disorders. The more parents and teachers know and work together the better they are at monitoring, managing and teaching students with ADHD (Vereb & DiPerna, 2004; and Bor, Sanders & Markie-Dadds, 2002). Future research promises to further improve diagnosis and intervention. The Multi-modal Treatment Study of ADHD (MTA) conducted by the National Institutes of Mental Health (1999) provides treatment strategies for children with ADHD. This landmark study for clinicians and researchers working with ADHD children recommends "carefully crafted" treatment.

This book is novel in that it promises one to take a look at ADHD as a unique style of behaving not merely a behavioral disorder. It offers simple and pragmatic ways to deal with a complex condition with an emphasis on the inclusion of non-medical interventions. A book of this nature is necessary to broaden the treatment spectrum of the ADHD presentation beyond the core symptoms of inattention, hyperactivity, and impulsivity. It is strongly suggested that one should address executive functions *first* and as *early* as possible in the development of a child.

This book started out as a textbook supplement for a course the author teaches in Psychopathology. In the author's practice of psychology, many third-party payers would request for the assessment/diagnosis of ADHD and the subsequent referral to a medical doctor for pharmacotherapy. In addition, the author conducts ADHD workshops to national and international teachers. Confession: This confluence of experience yielded much ambivalence—should it be a textbook or should it be a handbook for parents, teachers and counselors? In the final analysis, it became a combination that is practical and useful to whoever reads or uses it.

Chapter 1
What is ADHD?

It is common knowledge that individuals have experienced symptoms that resemble Attention Deficit Hyperactivity (ADHD) for decades and even centuries. The name, Attention Deficit Disorder, was first introduced in 1980 by a psychiatric team in the third edition of the Diagnostic and Statistical Manual of Mental Disorders (DSM-III). At different periods between this span of time, ADHD has been called many different names; a few include : Minimum Brain Dysfunction, Hyperkinetic Reaction of Children, and ADHD with or without Hyperactivity.

Attention Deficit Hyperactive Disorder is defined by some as a neurobiological (central nervous system) disorder (Barkley, 2005). Conrad (2006) indicates that ADHD is a developmental disorder estimated to range between 3 to 5 years. Attention Deficit Hyperactivity is chronic disorder that affects millions of children and often persists into adulthood (The Mayo Clinic Staff, 2009; Barkley, 1995, 2005). The DSM-IV-TR, (2000) provides criteria for three types. The types are ADHD, Predominantly Inattentive, ADHD, Predominantly Hyperactive-Impulsivity, and ADHD, Combined Type (the criteria described in detail later). The Inattentive type was formerly called Attention Deficit Disorder (ADD) and relegated to a residual place in the category of ADHD discussion. If the condition is not adequately and comprehensively addressed by parents, teachers, and mental health professionals, many different problems can result: school dropout, self medication and drug abuse, and behavioral disorders. What is needed is exposure to the knowledge and work; and to be aware of the time it takes to apply the data by all involved.

The Prevalence and the Sufferers of ADHD

Attention Deficit Hyperactivity Disorder is one of the most common childhood disorders reported to physicians and mental health professionals, by schools and parents. The DSM-IV-TR estimates the prevalence of ADHD to be between 3%-5% in school-age children. Studies have shown that the incidence of ADHD to be as high as 7.5 % (Barbaresa, 2002 at the Mayo Clinic; and Fine, 2002). By 1996, at least 40% of children referred to outpatient child psychiatry providers were diagnosed with ADHD (Austin, Reiss & Burgdorf, 2007). According to the Centers for Disease Control (CDC), 4.4 million youth between the ages of 4-17 have been diagnosed with the disorder.

Gender, race/ethnicity, and culture are also related to the incidence of ADHD. The condition is found more prevalently in boys than girls (DSM-IV-TR, 2002; Gershon & Gershon, 2002; Quinn, Wilens, & Spencer, 2004; Beiderman & Farvaone, 2004; and Zambo, 2008). Other documents report that the rate is about six times more prevalent among boys than among girls. Girls are diagnosed with the predominantly inattentive type of ADHD (Quinn, et al., 2004). They are underdiagnosed, misdiagnosed or diagnosed late due to shyness, being withdrawn or thought to be depressed (Beiderman & Faraone, 2004). Boys, on the other hand, are diagnosed most prevalently with the predominantly hyperactivity-impulsive and combined types. White males from affluent families make up the majority of children diagnosed with ADHD compared to Hispanics and African American males (Pastor, 2005; Havey, Olson, McCormick & Gates, 2005; and Samuel & Curtis, 1997).

In communities with a more multi-cultural population as in poor and rural areas, inner cities, barrios, and Native American reservations, the percentage may be overrepresented or underrepresented due to cultural, racial/ethnic, and economic factors (Williams, Swnson & Wigal, (1995). Attention Deficit Hyperactivity Disorder is probably found in all cultures but with differences in the incidence. Much research is needed in this area.

Broad Theories of Physical or Psychological Disorders

Research indicates that genetic, prenatal and perinatal, as well as, psychosocial factors may contribute to ADHD (Castellanos & Rapoport, 1992). Twin and other studies indicate that ADHD "runs in families" (Goodman & Stevenson, (1989). Zametkin (1995) described three cases: an eight-year-old boy, his father and his grandfather, who had ADHD. These cases pointed out that (a) ADHD is inherited; (b) it persists into adulthood; and (c) the intervention for children and adults are the same. Both biological and environmental factors have been suggested (Goldstein, 1996). Genetic, biochemical, neurobehavioral and neuroimaging studies suggest a neurological etiology for ADHD (Hynd, Hern, Voeller & Marshall, 1991).

Three theories explaining the etiology of medical and psychological disorder are the (1) diathesis-stress theory; (2) the genetics theory; and (3) a theory that deals with brain changes in individuals with ADHD. Most professionals believe that environmental factors play a causal role in the development of the disorders by interacting with genes. The diathesis-stress theory explains the development of any disorder as the interaction of both genetic and environmental factors.

Zentall (1983) suggests an optimal stimulation theory to account for ADHD. This theory suggests that individuals have a biologically determined optimal level of or arousal that they will work to maintain as environmental stimulation increases or decreases. The classical "overflow" theory of Strauss & Lehtinen (1947) indicate that hyperactive behavior is a reaction to a level of stimulation that exceeds processing capacity. One would react to a level of stimulation that exceeds processing capacity.

Neurological or brain changes of persons with ADHD are being studied in order to find a physical and/or chemical basis for the condition. Scientists want to know how the brain of persons with ADHD differ from that of persons without ADHD. They look at brain structure and size to correspond to ADHD symptoms. Likewise, researchers and drug companies look for neurotransmitters in the brain that correlate with symptoms of ADHD. A dopamine-catecholamine hypothesis involving neurotransmitters such as dopamine and norepinephrine (Castellanos & Rapoport, 1992; and serotonin (Goldstein, 1994) have been suggested as factors relating to ADHD. The right hemisphere and frontal lobes of the brain have been hypothesized as the locations of the biochemical causes of ADHD (Zametkin & Rapoport, 1987). The use of medications to treat ADHD constitutes the rationale for balancing the neurotransmitter responsible for some of the symptoms.

Before leaving the discussion of the theories concerning the causes of ADHD, it is informative to indicate that genes, the brain, and chemicals are related to everything about a human body and that experiences, the environment, or learning interact with the biological factors. Experiences can change each of these biological factors. A good analogy is that lifting weights changes the morphology of muscles with regular practice.

Types of ADHD and Criteria for Diagnosis

The DSM-IV-TR (2000) describes three subtypes of ADHD; they are ADHD, Predominantly Inattentive Type; ADHD, Predominantly Hyperactive-Impulsive Type; and ADHD, Combined Type. They are described verbatim. There are 18 criteria and the person must show at least six of the symptoms for a period of at least six months and first evident before the age of seven. In addition, the impairment from the symptoms must be present in at least two settings and must affect social, academic or occupational functioning. One must be able to make a differential diagnosis from other disruptive behaviors observed in Oppositional Defiant Disorder, Conduct Disorder, and Depression.

Criteria for the Predominantly Inattentive Type are as follows: (1) often does not seem to listen when spoken to directly; (2) often has difficulty sustaining attention in tasks or play activities; (3) often does not follow through on instructions and fails to finish schoolwork, chores or duties in the workplace (not due to oppositional behavior or failure to understand instructions); (4) often avoids, dislikes, or is reluctant to engage in tasks that require sustained mental effort (such a schoolwork or home work); (5) often loses things necessary for tasks or activities (e.g., toys, school assignments, pencils, books, or tools); (6) is often easily distracted by extraneous stimuli; (7) is often forgetful in daily activities. Criteria for the hyperactivity phase of the Predominantly Hyperactivity-Impulsivity Type are as follows:

(1) often fidgets with hands or feet or squirms in sea; (2) often leaves seat in classroom or in other situations in which remaining seated is expected; (3) often runs about or climbs excessively in situations in which it is inappropriate (in adolescents or adults, may be limited to subjective feelings of restlessness); (4) often has difficulty playing or engaging in leisure activities quietl; (5) is often "on the go" or often acts as if "driven by a motor;" and (6) often talks excessive. The criteria for the impulsivity phase of the Predominantly Hperactivity-Impulsivity Type are as follows: (1) often blurts out answers before questions have been completed; (2) often has difficulty awaiting turn; and (3) often interrupts or intrudes on others (e.g., butts into conversations or games)

Assessment and Diagnosis

Assessment or diagnosis is the most critical aspect of intervention for any type of disorder. Without appropriate diagnosis, inadequate or incorrect intervention will ensue. Individual practitioners may use their own unique assessment tools or battery. In the author's private practice, an in-depth, comprehensive battery of evaluation tools is used. The assessment is comprehensive enough to allow one to rule in or to rule out co-occurring disorders. They include the interview by the parents, primarily the mother, and the child depending on age, observations of the child, a rating scale for the parent and the teacher, intellectual assessment, assessment of achievement, and learning style. Neuropsychological assessment is added if the parents' interview suggests those kinds of deficits.

The diagnostic interview provides information about perinatal conditions of both herself and the developing fetus; delivery date information, as well as, early childhood health, environmental exposures and experiences such as falling or traumatic brain injuries. The diagnostic interview also yields hypotheses about diagnoses and possible formal tests that assist in ruling in/ ruling out co-morbid disorders. Tests of intellectual status will determine whether a person's grades are due to an intellectual factor, as well as, subtests that focus on attention deficits. Achievement tests will show a person's grade level correlates with one's intellect; and whether the two suggest a learning disability (LD). The behavior rating scales completed by the parent and teacher will show that the symptoms of ADHD are exhibited in at least two places. The learning style instrument will show the child's learning preferences and the conditions under which he will learn best. Co-morbid disorders must be ruled out and addressed, also. Parents can detect possible symptoms of ADHD early by noting the symptoms which occur during infancy in early childhood. If there are suspicions, parents should consult with a psychologist for further assessment and nondrug strategies.

Differential Diagnoses and Co-Morbid Disorders of ADHD

When co-morbid conditions are present, it can make the diagnosis of ADHD much more difficult to pinpoint and the symptoms harder to treat. Some co-morbid disorders that commonly occur alongside ADHD are Oppositional Defiant Disorder (ODD),Conduct Disorder (CD), Learning Disabilities (LD), Depression (D), Anxiet (Anx), the Bipolar Disorders (I and II), and Sensory Integration Disorder (Austin, e al., 2007). All disorders and symptoms discovered via the diagnostic process must be treated.

Symptoms of ADHD can be found in individuals with traumatic brain injury (TBI) or mental retardation (MR). Poor academic performance of students may be due to low intellectual level, low motivation, a learning disability, or the child is not being taught to his learning style. A child brought in for ADHD may have symptoms of Bipolar Disorder. Some parents while describing the behavior of their children will indicate that Their children behave similar to relatives with a Bipolar Disorder.

Chapter 2
If You Suspect Your Child Has ADHD?

Knowledge of the DSM-IV-TR criteria for the three types of ADHD in addition to early signs of ADHD observed in infants and preschool children will assist a parent in suspecting whether her child has ADHD. As noted earlier, prenatal behavior of the developing fetus can provide some information about its activeness. Symptoms of ADHD for infants are not in the DSM-IV-TR and are slightly different for preschool children. For infancy, they are (a) an aversion to being cuddled or held; (b) strained/negative mother-child relationship, and (c) more frequent crying. Symptoms for preschool children include (a) higher activity level than peers; (b) problems noticeable in structured play; (c) aggressive behavior; (c) difficulty going to sleep; (e) motor restlessness during sleep; (f) strong will "difficult to manage"; and (g) family disorganization and parents feeling overwhelmed (Austin, Reiss & Burgdorf (2007). Individuals with the Inattentive Type of ADHD (primarily females) are seen as reserved, lady-like, shy or even depressed, and their academic performance is poor. It used to be called Attention Deficit Disorder (ADD), relegated to an important place in the DSM manual, and often missed in females.

A typical example is that of a mother who brought her high-school-age daughter in for psychological treatment because her grades were declining (I must emphasize that her grades were declining). The diagnostic workup revealed that she had ADHD although she presented with symptoms of depression. The young lady remarked, "I have been telling you that I needed to see a counselor since elementary school. This was a quiet, demure and talented student who had gone undetected for ADHD for years. In too many cases, the only time a child is brought in for counseling is when grades are declining.

A child with ADHD does not behave the way other children during the same age or developmental level in the three core areas of ADHD—inattentiveness, hyperactivity, and impulsivity. Parents may observe their children exhibiting sleep problems as infants, memory problems if school age, and academic problems at school. In addition, teachers may be sending home notes about disruptive behaviors in the classroom.

Teachers are usually the most frequent referral source of children with ADHD, parents are usually the second most frequent individuals who refer students to either psychologist or a medical professional. In most cases, parents take their children to a medical professional based on what they observe and from complaints by teachers instead of obtaining a diagnostic workup by a psychologist first. There needs to be more than a 15-minute office visit for the assessment and diagnosis of ADHD (University of Michigan Health System (UMHS) Guideline for Clinical Care for ADHD 2005). This leads to the need for a comprehensive and indepth diagnostic workup that is done by a psychologist or appropriately trained-mental health counselor. Third-party payers need to realize this and pay for a complete assessment before medical or psychological intervention is initiated.

What Do Parents Do?

Parents bring their children to a psychologist when there is a decline in grades which occurs as a result of the ADHD symptoms. In many cases, it is academic decline not symptoms of ADHD or other psychological or behavioral problems that get parents concerned. It is as if academic decline is a barometer of things not going well with their children. Ideally, a DSM-diagnostic workup should be done when ADHD is first suspected and before medical or psychological interventions are recommended or initiated. A comprehensive diagnostic workup is one which will include both psychological disorders (which may be co-morbid disorders) and medical disorders which will need to be treated first. The DSM-IV-TR (2000) diagnosis has Axes which include both psychiatric disorders (Axis I), medical disorders (Axis III), psychosocial factors (Axis IV) the child may be experiencing, and how well the child is functioning (Axis V). Axis II Disorders include Mental Retardation and Personality Disorders.

What Psychologists Do?

A psychologist engages in a comprehensive data-gathering process with various assessment instruments to place on the five DSM-IV-TR axes. The instruments usually include the diagnostic interview, observation checklist, rating scales by the parent and the teacher, a test of intellectual ability, an academic achievement test, and a learning style measure. If other disorders are suspected such as anxiety, depression, or bipolar disorders, or neuropsychological deficits, additional instruments are administered. The interview provides background information dealing with development, illnesses, and early childhood experiences. The interview also suggests other assessment tools that need to be administered to rule in/out. Observations by the psychologists can support some of the behaviors reported in the interview. Rating scales by the parent and teacher are based on observations at home and at school (the criteria suggests that the disorder needs to occur in at least two places).

The psychologist needs to know whether poor academic performance is due to intellectual level, or a learning disability (LD). The I.Q. and the achievement tests can assist in making that determination. The learning style instrument is administered to determine the conditions under which the child learns best. After the diagnostic workup, a psychologist begins intervention plans which include psychological intervention, school or classroom intervention, family work, and a medical referral. Other recommendations may include psychoeducation and support, parent skills training, ADHD support groups, social skills training, cognitive behavioral therapy, and school consultation and intervention (UMHS, 2005; and Ianelli, 2008). The American Academy of Pediatrics (AAP) states that a care plan for children with ADHD should include psychological intervention along with any other prescribed medications (2001).

The bottom line is that any conclusion should be based on the knowledge that ADHD begins in early childhood and persists throughout adulthood. The intervention should be individualized and specific to the symptoms that are presented. This is probably the rationale for developing an individual education plan (IEP). The plan should include one's unique learning style. Helping professionals, parents and teachers should be "on the same page" and have the same goals for the child. The goals of intervention should focus on executive function, the core symptoms, and peripheral problems such as social problems, low self esteem, and memory problems. All parents want their children to be safe, be able to control their behaviors, and to function independently. A recommendation is that medication be considered as part of the treatment with either behavioral stimulants, antidepressants, antipsychotics, antihypertensives, or anti-anxiety agents depending on the type of ADHD, the individual set of symptoms, co-morbid disorders, and body chemistry.

Multidisciplinary Collaboration Effort

There should never be competition among the various disciplines and professionals when it comes to helping children, including children and adolescents with ADHD. Occasionally, it appears that everyone is not "on the same page." Sometimes, a father and a mother may not be together. In the practice of the author, seldom does the father visit the psychologist with the mother and the child. When a father does accompany the pair, he objects to being there and disagrees with the treatment whether it is medical or psychological. Sometimes, parents may not work collaboratively with the teacher; and a medical professional may minimize or reject information or suggestions from a non-medical professional. Professionals do their job but may work in isolation with each other. The goal here is to emphasize the effectiveness of collaboration in treatment.

Teachers usually send parents information about the behavior of their children, parents should approach a diagnostician to do a comprehensive workup with a treatment plan and medical referrals to a physician (psychiatrist, pediatrician or a primary care physician). Many physicians will refer a child to a diagnostician before prescribing medicine; others will prescribe medicine and then refer to a diagnostician. If a medicine is prescribed before a diagnostician does a workup, the physician should strongly consider consultation with an appropriate specialist (UMHS ADHD Guideline, 2005). All professionals and the parents should work collaboratively and consult with each other on a regular basis in implementing and monitoring progress of the child. The communication of all involved can be enhanced with electronic tools. A lot of time is spent by both parents and teachers with a child with ADHD. It is suggested that the same amount of time can be spent in different ways and with different strategies. The use of electronic tools of communication and the use of new strategies and approaches may reduce the amount of time.

Chapter 3:
The Medical Approach

Medication has its role in the treatment of psychological conditions. A book on non-drug treatment of ADHD does not preclude the use of medicine when needed or decided on by adults and guardians of children. To do so would be going against the guidelines for treating ADHD set by AAP (2001) and UMHS (2005) and other entities. Medication is not a cure for ADHD (UMHS, 2005) but it alleviates or abates some symptoms of ADHD, but not other symptoms (NIMH Report (1996). All medicines have therapeutic effects, side effects, and adverse effects. Individuals on medications should read the labels about the effects, consult with the prescribing physicians by reporting back to them frequently, and complying with the medical regimen. Some clients or parents of children will stop taking a medication abruptly rather than allowing the physician to gradually take them off a drug if that is appropriate, modify the drug or change to another drug. There is the potential that adolescents may abuse the drug or use other drugs with the prescribed drug.

Unlike learning approaches, the effects of medications are transient and varies according to individual characteristics (age, weight, health) and type of drug (behavioral stimulant, antidepressant, antipsychotics). The Food and Drug Administration, FDA, (2007; 2005) directed ADHD drug manufacturers to develop patient medication guides to alert patients to possible cardiovascular risks and risks of adverse psychiatric symptoms associated with the medicines, and to advise them of precautions that can be taken. The use of drugs can be dangerous, but not under the monitoring and supervision of the prescribing physician (Chandler, 2002).

Prescription Drugs to Treat ADHD

In some cases, when ADHD is not addressed appropriately (i.e., when an individual is not assessed, diagnosed, and referred to a psychologically-oriented physician), the individual may self-medicate with illicit drugs or a legal drug such as alcohol. If drug abuse is a problem in teenagers, short-short-acting stimulants may not be used (Chandler, 2002). Parents may delay a medical referral; this choice could allow a condition to worsen or have a greater negative impact on academic performance and life, in general. When this is a choice, it creates more problems than previously.

The most frequently prescribed category of medication, as well as, first-line treatment for ADHD is the behavioral stimulants. A few examples of behavioral stimulants include methylphenidate (Ritalin, Concerta, Metadate, Datran), dextroamphetamine (Dextostat, Dexedrene), metamphetamine (Desoxyn), and lisdexamfetamine (Vyvanse). Other medications used to treat ADHD include drugs that are non-stimulants such as Straterra. Other non-stimulants include antidepressants such as selective serotonin reuptake inhibitors (SSRIs), monoamine oxidase inhibitors (MOAIs) and trycyclics (TCAs); antipsychotic medicines; antianxiety agents (Maidment, 2003; Waxmonsky, 2005; and Biedmerman, Wilens, Steingard & Geist, 2007); and antihypertensives (clonidine (Catapress) and mood stabilizers such as valporic acid. According to treatment guidelines, some of the non-stimulants are used when behavioral stimulants are ineffective or co-morbid disorders are present (UMHS, 2005).

The behavioral stimulants are usually prescribed for ADHD, Predominantly Hyperactive- Type and the Combined Type; but when the diagnosis, ADHD, is given, behavioral stimulants are usually prescribed. Antidepressant medications are prescribed for ADHD, Predominantly Inattentive Type of ADHD. These medications may include tricyclic antidepressants (imipramine, desipramine; monoamine oxidase inhibitors; and the selective norepinephrine transporter inhibitor atomoxetine (Straterra).

Children with ADHD are usually placed on medications during the school hours only and not in the evenings, on weekends or during the summer months (a "drug holiday"). This practice is usually carried out to compensate for reduced growth of individuals on behavioral stimulants. Again, this is a choice that parents make as to whether they want their children placed on the behavioral stimulations at times other than the school day.

Different Effects of Drugs

Drugs have therapeutic effects, side effects, and adverse effects. Parents and teachers need to know the different kinds of effects on children. Therapeutic effects are those that eliminate symptoms of the child; no drug will eliminate all symptoms. Side effects are those effects that interfere with the functioning of a child such as sleep and appetitie, effect on the heart, bladder control, worsen the symptoms or cause a child to act like a zombie (UMHS, 2005). Adverse effects are severe effects that may act opposite to the therapeutic effects, irreversible and may be fatal. A person using the prescribed drug may use other drugs simultaneously and yield interaction effects (undermedication or overmedication). A person may use illicit or over-the-counter drugs in combination and produce dangerous effects.

It is wise for parents to determine what the specific therapeutic effects of a drug are on their children. Guidelines in the literature indicate that behavioral stimulants have a reducing effect on the core symptoms of ADHD (inattentiveness, hyperactivity and impulsivity). Side effects include appetite suppression and weight losss, sleep difficulties, depression and sometimes suicidal ideation, and cardiovascular disorders (FDA, 2007). Stratera, a non-psychostimulant, may increase attention and control hyperactivity and impulsivity (Ianelli, 2005). Antidepressants such as the trycyclics reduce hyperactivity, impulsiveness, anxiety and moodiness; but not recommended for persons with cardiac problems. The antidepressant buproprion (Welbutrin) reduces hyperactivity and aggression but seizure disorders and eating disorders are contraindicated. Antihypertensive drugs such as clonidine (Catapres) and guanfacine (Tenex) reduce hypertensiveness, impulsiveness and aggression. Tenex will help a person with sleep problems when taken in combination with a behavioral stimulant. These are 2nd-line drugs and have not been approved by FDA (Ianelli, 2005).

It cannot be overemphasized that a person on medications should allow their physician to monitor and manage their medications. They know the category of medicines and conditions under which medicines are prescribed based on their own medical history intake and data from the diagnostic professional. Chandler (2002) indicated that a condition in which medications should be given is when children with ADHD are experiencing changes in their lives such as divorce, parents' remarriages, and moving to new schools. In some cases, medicines, especially the behavioral stimulants, have received a bad name due to misuse, abuse or abruptly stopping the use a medication.

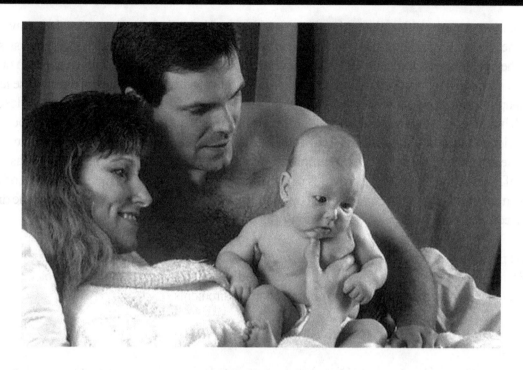

Chapter 4
The Non-Medical Approach

Guidelines on treatment of children with ADHD indicate that management of the disorder includes not only drugs but (a) psychoeducation; (b) parent skill training; (c) family therapy; (d) ADHD support group; (e) social skills training; (f) cognitive behavioral therapy; (g) school consultation and intervention; and (h) alternative complimentary treatment (Hechtman, Hinshaw, Pelham, & Swanson (1995); AAP, 2001; UMHS, 2005; and Ianelli, 2008). These treatment guidelines are comprehensive to include the education of parents and all professionals—teachers, counselors and other mental health professionals, and physicians. A knowledge of community resources are also required by all concerned. Behavioral therapies, cognitive therapies, education plans are a few non-drug interventions that are required to offer effective intervention in treating ADHD in children and adolescents. Each non-drug strategy includes an element of learning except alternative complimentary treatments, which involve vitamins, herbs and other ingested products.

Learning is a relatively permanent change in behavior. The effects of these non-drug approaches are relatively permanent, if they are put into practice. Additionally, there are few, if any, side effects. The approaches and strategies will require changes with age and grade level such as time management, social skills, and self monitoring. The present author emphasizes the use of these approaches and activities early in age and grade level. By the time the child is an adolescent, they will have acquired time management and social skills.

One must comply with and practice the procedures and behaviors taught so that they may become relatively permanent and routine. Parents, teachers and professional helpers can assist with the development and maintenance of new effective behaviors. Parents have reasons to protest the use of medication for their children if the reason is that the drug is ineffective, due to dose level, and inappropriate drug choice or misdiagnosis. Usually, a physician may begin with a low dose which has no effect and increases the dose to determine if an effect in reducing symptoms occurs. If a dose is too much, a student can become lethargic and drowsy. Teachers and parents have indicated that they prefer the ADHD symptoms than to see a child lethargic due to an increased dose of medication. The author provides psychoeducation for the parents to report effects of a drug on the child to give the physician the opportunity to change the dose level or change the drug for effectiveness. If no drug works then non-drug therapies are the only choices.

The present writer prefers to conceptualize ADHD disorders either as complex or as a syndrome rather than a unitary disorder. There are individual differences, multiple problems associated with it, and multidisciplinary intervention requirements.

Addressing Problems with Executive Functions and ADHD

Attention Deficit Hyperactivity Disorders are associated with deficits in executive functions (EFs), organizational problems, memory, and social interactions, in addition to the core problems of inattentiveness, hyperactivity, and impulsivity. Executive functions are a collection of varying abilities that involve a set of cognitive abilities that control and regulate other abilities and behaviors necessary for goal-directed behavior (Encyclopedia of Mental Health, 2009; Denby, 2008; Brown, 2003; and Lesaca, 2001). Brown (2003) compares EF to the director of an orchestra managing and controlling all sections.

Executive functions include the ability to initiate and stop actions, to monitor and change behavior as needed, to plan future behavior when faced with novel tasks and situations, allows one to anticipate outcomes and adapt to changing situations, and the ability to form concepts and think abstractly.

According to Lesaca (2001) the major executive functions are as follows:

- Response inhibition which permits impulse control, resistance to distraction, and delay of gratification;
- Nonverbal working memory which permits holding of events in the mind and allows self-awareness across time;
- Verbal working memory which comprises the internalization and permits self description, questioning, and reading comprehension; and
- Self-regulation of emotion and motivation which permits motivation, persistence toward a goal, and emotional self control.

There appears to be a consensus that EFs are central cognitive processes. The range of cognitive processes include storing and retrieving memory, organization enhancement, controlling/ regulating social behaviors, planning for the future, inhibiting/stopping behaviors, initiating/starting behaviors, monitoring/regulating information, sustaining attention, and modifying motor behavior (Packer, 1998; Dendy, 2002; National Center for Learning Disabilities, 2009).

Cognitive processes involve the prefrontal and frontal cortices and connecting sub-cortical structures. The frontal lobe region of the cerebral cortex allows for the creation and execution of difficult tasks (O'Reily, 2007). The frontal lobe is critical for efficient functioning in daily life and develops gradually through childhood (Anderson, Jacobs & Anderson, 2008). Prefrontal executive dysfunction results in impaired regulation of cognition, attention, behaviors, arousal, and emotion, all of which have serious and pervasive consequences for functioning across the life span. These executive function deficits are typically difficult to treat, ameliorate, or remediate and require sensitive handling by caretakers. Executive dysfunction can arise as a consequence of many different factors—metabolic, genetic, certain types of epilepsy, prematurity, traumatic brain injury, hypoxia, and toxic exposure (Powell & Voeller (2004).

The brain is a dynamic organ that can change morphologically, but not in the number of cells. Indications are that brain-based and cognitive enhancement programs can increase many of the skills and components of EF if they are initiated in early childhood. It is suggested that if strategies are directed toward executive functions at the outset, some of the core problems are alleviated, thus the rationale for addressing EFs first and other problems subsequently. The environment and early experiences of children reared in poor homes versus those in more economically enhanced environments play a role in the development of EFs (Bussing, Shoenberg & Perwein, 1998). It is never too late to address problems, but earlier the better.

Measures of and Strategies to Improve Executive Functions

Since executive functions are high-level abilities that influence several different aspects and processes, problems with EF make it difficult to assess all of these processes singly. There are memory scales of measurement; subscales on the Wechsler Intelligence tests that measure working memory and processing speed; and Trails A and Trails B which is a measure of executive control and cognitive flexibility (Arbuthnott & Frank, 2000). There are several other neuropsychological tools that measure specific components of EF.

Knowledge of developmental psychology indicates that teaching and other experiences are more effective when started early and when a child is maturationally ready. The brain's executive functions begin to develop in early childhood as the prefrontal cortex develops, then continue through adolescence into young adulthood (Brown, 2003). Early childhood is an optimal period of time to assess some of the processes of EF and to initiate intervention strategies. Some parents do not know what to look for in infancy and early childhood and cannot begin intervention early. Other parents may overlook, deny, and wait until the child begins to do poorly in schoolor before initiating intervention strategies. Some parents and even professionals may not be familiar with the major EF functions described by Lasaca (2001) listed above. Early intervention during preschool includes relaxation activities, safety instructions, and role playing prosocial behaviors such as taking turns to speak or not breaking lines. At school-age, both parents and teachers may continue to use strategies that help students improve EF such as training students how to make and use checklists, showing them how to use time and material organizers, and the use of mnemonic devices. As early as possible, but especially in adolescents, allow the use of electronic devices which the author calls "prosthetics." Prosthetics are those tools, gadgets and electronic devices used to assist and enhance the development of EF and performance. Metzer (2007) also emphasizes the use of important ideas, concepts, and strategies for remembering.

Meltzer (2007) takes these strategies a step further from the book, *Executive Function in Education,* by suggesting memorization, cognitive flexibility, prioritizing, note taking, and self-monitoring. Memorization is more effective if mnemonic devices such as the use of rhymes, jokes and music are used. Cognitive therapy techniques to make flexible cognitions by requiring thinking in alternative ways to solve a problem. Set up exercises for students demonstrating how past experiences can be can be used in new situations. Teach students how to monitor and evaluate themselves. Any time a student has seat work at home or at school, the parent or teacher should require the student to develop the habit of checking their work before someone else checks it (UMHS, 2005). Always reinforce these efforts.

Bottom line: Students with ADHD may have common symptoms; however, there are individual differences in the clinical picture of individuals with the disorders. One needs to focus on those symptoms that are unique to the child or student and develop or use strategies for that child.

Addressing Problems of Inattention

If a child is not paying attention, information is not received and there is no information to be stored, processed and acted upon. Input, process, and output are the components that must take place during learning and acting on that learning. The process component entails selecting stimuli to act upon. Children need practice in listening and following directions based on what they have heard. Provide frequent listening exercises in following directions in increasing levels of background noise. Parents are instructed to have their child practice listening techniques about five minutes a day. When talking to a child with ADHD, make sure there is eye contact and the opportunity to repeat several times what has been heard and understood. Older children may paraphrase what they have heard and taught to use "self talk", a cognitive therapy technique. These techniques are usually taught in therapy with the parents for them to carry out at home. *In vivo* exercises can be very effective. Use the techniques whenever you are talking to the child.

Providing short, specific assignments will increase the probability of students receiving, storing and acting on information appropriately. Likewise, providing instructions that are precise and clear-cut will ensure that a student follow directions better. It is frequently recommended that children are given one set of instructions rather than multiple instructions to carry out. Reinforce the child for his efforts and success.

Any technique or procedure to reduce distractibility in the classroom or workplace is one of the most highly recommended approaches to impact the problem of inattention. This can be done by reducing distractions in the number of materials on the walls and bulletin boards usually found in classrooms or one's life. Distractions can also be reduced by gradually adding materials on the boards and putting the distraction such as color into the material rather than on the walls or bulletin boards. As information is gradually added to bulletin boards; other information is gradually removed to prevent the feeling of being overwhelmed or confused. High stimulus clothing and jewelry that some Kindergarten and elementary teachers often wear can be a source of distraction for some students who are diagnosed with ADHD.

At least 25 percent of desks in the classroom should be cubicles so that students who are easily distracted may use them when doing seat work or taking a tests. Some students may benefit further by using earplugs while doing important seatwork or taking tests. Inattention or distractibility accounts for the inability to complete assignments or getting started in the first place. A cue may be used to get them started along with a stopwatch to time them when they get started on their work. The stopwatch can aid in getting students to end their work quicker and quicker each time. To keep the child on target and to complete his work, divide the material in small segments and allow them to take breaks with the idea that they must return to complete the work. Keep in mind that it may take several breaks before the work is completed. Reinforce the child for each completed segment as soon as possible so that the child can see a beginning and an end of a task. Whatever a teacher does or provides in her classroom to maintain attention of a child with ADHD should not bring attention to that child. A general statement can be made to all students that if they are distracted they may use earplugs, cubicles or other devices. The manner in which a teacher manages the behavior and teaches a child with ADHD has implications for the child's self esteem and the perceptions peers have about that child.

A frequent observation of some students with ADHD is their tendency to be perfect; this tendency to turn out perfect work interferes with the completion their tasks. These perfectionistic tendencies present themselves by students writing painstakingly slow in an effort to write perfectly. Often when work is not perceived as being perfect it is thrown away and the work is begun again. When this is the case, allow the student to complete the entire assignment without erasing or placing the partial work in the trash can and starting again. On the other end of the spectrum, there are individuals who hurriedly complete their work resulting in many errors. Encourage and allow this type of student to check her work before turning it in.

Some of the same techniques that are used for the individual that is slow in getting started can be used effectively. They include dividing work into small segments, taking frequent breaks at the end of the segments, and immediate reinforcement for success in completing each segment or the entire task. The use of technology can be incorporated in the process by allowing individuals to check their own work before handing it in. Individuals at the adolescent or adult stage are recommended to engage in many of the strategies and techniques used with children. It is recommended that students with ADHD be given more time if needed. As teachers and parents, you would want to know if the child can do the work not how fast. If the child had just been given more time, the grade could have been higher. One can work on speed after determining whether the child knows the material.

Address*ing* Symptoms of Hyperactivity

Since the students are very active and on the move, capitalize on their mobility by involving the student in learning tasks requiring activity and movement when possible. Some students with ADHD can comprehend what they read better if they are walking the hallway while they read. The Dunn & Dunn learning styles model would recommend that a teacher or parent make plans to use mobility and kinesthetic activities and tactile materials during a lesson for highly active students. Another way to capitalize on the need to be mobile and active is to use psychodrama (the author calls it psycho-dramatizing the content/lesson). Other strategies to use for a learner that has a high need for mobility are to make "hopscotch" games out of a learning segment; integrate field trips; and use tactual-hands-on materials in teaching.

Permit the entire class to take breaks between segments of work; giving them the opportunity to chat with friends (could be about the lesson), get a drink of water or snack, and visit the bathroom or stretch. After the break, a cue is given to quiet down and resume a task. There are some activities from which the entire class can benefit; use appropriately and as often as possible. If the entire class is involved, no undue attention or negative perceptions are directed toward the student with ADHD.

Identical or the same procedure suggested can be used at home as well as at school or work. Mid-morning and mid-afternoon recesses would be better than a nap for a child with ADHD. One could plan a musical or dance activity either for the break or in place of a nap. Parents have reported the futile efforts of teachers trying to get a child with ADHD to take a nap. If successful, they are unable to sleep at night and arise on time.

Research on a condition called scotopic sensitivity syndrome indicates that fluorescent lighting often found in classrooms and offices affect individuals by making them restless; studying in dim or dark rooms or wearing prescribed tinted lenses helps in quieting them down (Irlen, 1983). The work of Irlen and the Dunns would recommend incandescent, dim, or natural lighting in classrooms for some students or individuals at work. Fluorescent lights are used primarily in schools and in businesses and are economical as well as "green", but this segment of the population needs to be accommodated with incandescent or natural lighting. Intermittent reinforcements of various types (i.e. tokens, social, privileges) for time-on task and time-in seat (and other behaviors) should be used whenever necessary to reduce hyperactivity.

Addressing Symptoms of Impulsivity

Impulsivity is characterized by speaking out of turn, not waiting their turn in line, and not thinking before one speaks or behaves. In other words, the individual acts on the spur of the moment or is impatient. This behavior can be dangerous in some cases when a child runs out in the street for a ball before thinking and looking. Some years ago, a parent was observed with a leash on her child. She later learned that this was to keep her child from running into the street downtown. Teaching the child early and providing practice early in life can substitute for the leash.

A student may rush through their seatwork assignments or tests and make many errors. This problem can be corrected with the use of cognitive-behavioral therapy techniques. The parent, teacher, or counselor may require the student to think of two or three ways to do a task before it is done. Give the child exercises in making plans for doing a task before actually doing them. In addition, ask students for ideas about the consequences or results of behaving one way or another. A child can be taught to say "let me think about it" when asked to give a response or to do something then give them time to think about it. Ask them what they came up with after they have thought about it and then praise them for the process.

A parent and a teacher can set an example for students. Many students imitate what parents and models do more readily than what they say. Social psychology tells us that learning by imitation is an effective procedure. Cognitive-behavioral therapy can assist a person with impulsive behaviors; the procedures can be taught to either the parents or the child. For those students who rush through their work, require them to check their own work before turning it in or before having someone else to check it. The activities described teach children to develop executive functions that are required in thinking and planning.

Social Skills Intervention

The application of social learning research on modeling or imitation has been suggested as a tool in dealing with inappropriate behaviors. Learning by imiatation can, again be applied for social skills learning. The therapist can model appropriate behaviors and teach the same to parents and others who work with the child at home. The same can be taught to teachers in a consultative model. The child with ADHD can observe and practice waiting their turn, sharing, asking for help, responding to negative situations like teasing, then allow the child to practice. Give the child practice in "reading" the facial expressions and gestures of other people. Teach the individual how his or her behavior affects others and teach new prosocial behaviors.

Psychoeducation of peers are also appropriate to engage in and is a totally novel approach to addressing the social skills of individuals with ADHD. What this strategy entails is teaching individuals how to understand their own behaviors, as well as, the behaviors of others. In other words, teach *all* students about individual differences and how to respect differences in others, as well, as different ways of interpreting the behavior of others. For example, if a child with ADHD touches his classmate, the classmate may interpret the touch as a "hitting" response and the intention to be bothersome. The child who is touched may yell out that child X hit him and child X gets sent to the office or is reprimanded in other ways. This scenario affects self esteem and the perception of the child's classmates. The way this is handled can result in peers disliking the person with ADHD.

A teacher needs to understand the social nature of the child with ADHD and the innate need to touch without the intent of being disruptive or bothersome; and give different interpretations to the touching. An alternative interpretation is that the child with ADHD is friendly or wants to be a friend. One needs to be able to make the distinction between touching to be friendly and when touching is the result of aggression, a product of frustration and address each appropriately. Teaching other students how to behave and think toward the behavior of a person with ADHD does not mean that the teacher and parents would not teach him how to manage touching and ways others can interpret his behavior. Teaching goes both ways. The author remembers when parents reared or taught their children to not make fun of persons who were different from them and to not laugh at people who had deformities or speech problems. Our society has deviated from that kind of teaching these days.

Much of what has been discussed is social skills training and what others such as teachers can say and do to change the attitude of students in the class about a person who may have ADHD. Research indicates that sociometric data reveals that children with ADHD are not liked and have few friends. Once a child with ADHD has been rejected, it is difficult to overcome the perception. It is recommended that medication and behavioral or social skills training be applied. Medication can be effective at reducing negative behaviors that peers find aversive, whereas social skills and behavioral interventions teach and reinforce prosocial skills (Hoza, 2006).

Addressing Memory Problems and ADHD

We all have walked in another room to get something and could not remember what he went for. In situations such as this, one could engage in what Albert Ellis calls "self talk" which is repeating to one's self what they are going to obtain or do. The child should be trained to not stop on the way to do something else (i.e., not get distracted). Memory can be enhanced by coaching the child to make a list of items or events that come to mind as they are thought of during the week. A parent can do the same with their grocery list on a computer, memory board or posted on the refrigerator as a model for the child. Many people engage in this ritual. Is it due to ADHD, too many things on on one's mind or multitasking to save time? It does not matter; people still forgot what they started out to get or to do. It is common knowledge that the use of mnemonic devices are effective in helping to enhance memory. These are techniques that can be taught to individuals with ADHD and other children. The more techniques and accommodations there are for all children, the less attention is drawn to the person with ADHD.

According to Andries (2006), there are tips that a teacher can use to increase memory in ADHD students. Some of the tips used to help an ADHD student to retain what is being taught are as follows:

- Face the student when talking to them
- Use a signal when something is important.
- Vary the tone of voice.
- Use a soft voice when giving directions.
- Pause and create suspense by looking around before asking questions.
- Randomly pick readers so students cannot time their attention.
- Repeat and paraphrase.
- Shorten lessons that call for sustained attention.
- Use a pointer to indicate materials on the blackboard if you want students to focus.
- Write key concepts on the board and repeat them. Use visual aids.
- Have children to repeat questions before answering.
- Actively involve students.
- Randomly pick readers so students cannot time their attention.
- Allow students to doodle or use fidgeters (stress balls, coloring books, etc.).

Parents and tutors can also use the same tips. One can readily see that some of the tips are designed to assist a student in remembering what is being taught by getting attention, maintaining attention, and making the learning material short. Other tips involves the student in the learning activity; this aids the student in learning in all parts or more than one part of the body. Repeating information and paraphrasing it is making use of different parts of the brain. Other tips keep the learner alert and waiting or wondering whether the teacher is going to call on her next.

Other tips, this author calls "prosthetics." Other children wear glasses, hearing aids or use wheelchairs. Persons with ADHD can also use prosthetics: wear watches, use stop watches or talking clocks, timers, appointment books, computers, and note pads. According to Hebb's memory work years ago, individuals also need time for information to reverberate (to consolidate and pass from sensory memory to short-term memory and to long-term memory). Give children longer periods of time to complete a task (i.e., use distributed practice rather than massed practice). Some parents pressure their children to sit for hours and not move until they are all done with homework (mass practice) rather than allowing and encouraging them to take breaks between work periods (distributed practice).

Addressing Organizational Problems and ADHD

Children with ADHD experience problems with time and material organization. Children have not organized time well when they wait until the last minute to do tasks such as homework (procrastination). They have not organized time well if they spend hours and hours on homework. Parents tell the author that their children go to bed late due to the long hours it takes to do homework and may be late rising the next morning.

Time management is how your child keeps up with homework assignments, activities, and appointments (Goldberg, 2004). It deals with beginning tasks, ending tasks and being on time. Time management for young children can be taught, as well as, the use of audible stop watches, clocks and other gadgets or tools. Train individuals to set their watches 10 or 15 minutes fast and assume that this is the correct time to prevent them from being late. Individuals should be taught to live by time devices ranging from calendars to electronic devices. They are excellent in serving as prompts especially when a child becomes hyperfocused and spends too much time on one task. Teach the child to ask himself questions and become self mangers.

Problems with material organization are shown when the child's room or desk or locker is messy. The child cannot find what is needed to carry out a task, such as tools and assignments or he may forget to bring a jacket home. Children can be taught to perform activities or duties immediately such as making his bed. Do not reinforce procrastination. Encourage immediate performance and practice until doing the procedure becomes routine. Children can write a list of things to be done in order for the day each night before bed time or in the morning. Eventually, plans should be made for a week. Again, the use of a calendar or an appointment book can be useful.

According to Boller (2008), organizational skills are seen from a developmental perspective and that middle school students need support and instructions before they can improve on their organizational skills. The present author suggests that coaching, setting examples, and giving instructions beginning at an earlier age or grade levels are effective organizational teaching. At home, require children to have a place for everything and assist in building a routine and remembering where items are placed. These same behaviors will be generalized in other places. At school, teachers may allow time for *all* students to clean out their desks, notebooks, backpacks, and lockers. It is highly recommended that teachers and parents are "on the same page" and will work together with items to be brought back and forth to school. In most classes, only one or two students have ADHD in a classroom; therefore, teachers are not sending notes back and forth for many students. Teachers and parents are already spending time chastising a student with ADHD, it is a matter of using the time differently. In the long run, the student can manage himself without close monitoring from others.

Chapter 5
The Learning Style Approach to Address ADHD Problems

A psychologist, and to some extent, a mental health counselor, is trained to see psychopathology (illness) and will focus on weaknesses and will apply the deficit and remediation models. Mental health professionals may emphasize changing the child with ADHD rather than focusing on strength and changing the environment when appropriate. The fact is that some individual traits possessed by persons with ADHD cannot be changed even though some parents will punish their children as if they could. In some cases, changing the environment and adapting the environment to the learner is the best path to take. The various learning style (LS) theories are educational and they stress teaching students according to their LS and/or accommodating their needs. Psychologists and psychiatrists see ADHD as a mental disorder; LS theorists see individuals with ADHD as possessing a strong need to move (kinesthetic), touch things and people (tactual), and to talk excessively. Learning style theorists and practitioners indicate that parents, teachers, and tutors need to teach the students according to their style of learning and engaging in other activities of living.

There are several (LS) models; the Dunn & Dunn model has been the most heuristic. Rita Dunn supervised 164 dissertations, Personal Communications, April 1, 2009). Learning style knowledge, skills and practice are based on over 110 research articles and books by the Dunns and colleagues dating as far back as 1972 (Dunn & Dunn, 1972). They have sponsored training institutes; and developed learning style assessment instruments (Dunn, Dunn & Price (1975, 1979, 1985, 1987, 1989). The techniques and strategies described below emanate from training in LS, assessing the

LS of both students and clients, and treating ADHD clients from third grade to college level since 1992. The LS profile shows the learning preferences of an individual in 22 elements within five categories of stimuli. They are environmental, emotional, sociological, physical and psychological. The information below describes the preferences and conditions under which a person with ADHD will learn best when information is new and/or difficult; and how to teach and manage them in a learning setting.

Environmental Stimuli (Sound, light, temperature and design)

1. Sound

Individuals with Attention Deficit Hyperactivity Disorder (ADHD) are easily distractible by light, sound, and other stimuli that may not be noticed by others. Engage in the following according to the symptoms presented by the individual student.

   a. Provide quiet environment, or use soft background music to drown out distractions.

   b. Permit the use of headphones or earplugs or background music to block out distractions.

   c. Allow music or white noise for those students who are not bothered by sound/noise and appear to either tune it out or it is somehow enhancing.

   d. Keep a portion of the room free of obvious auditory distractions.

   e. Seat student next to smart and quiet peers (especially quiet girls).

   f. Play music without words (e.g., classical or baroque music quietly in the background or white noise while students are working.

   g. Provide a quiet, carpeted space in the room as a special study section for independent reading or use indoor/outdoor carpeting throughout the entire room.

   h. Use sound to relate directly to the material to be learned.

   i. Change your voice level and variation in word pacing to increase attention.

2. Light

Fluorescent lights produce adverse effects on individuals with ADHD; apparently they can detect the minute vibrations which make them more hyperactive; other sources of bright light are distracting.

   a. Allow students/individuals to wear caps with bibs to reduce the intensity of light.

b. Allow students to wear tinted lenses/glasses (prescribed or sunglasses) in class.

c. Allow students/individual to use colored overlays over reading materials.

d. Allow students/individuals to sit near windows, if not distracting, or on the side of the room where the lights are not on.

e. Allow students/individuals to highlight reading materials.

f. Use buff-colored paper rather than white if the room lighting creates glare on white paper.

3. Temperature

Individuals with ADHD often pull off some of their clothing as a sweater and because they prefer cool temperature.

a. Provide comfortable temperature in the room as best you can.

b. Allow students to dress comfortably (e.g., pull off/put on a sweater).

c. Allow students to drink water (i.e., make frequent trips to the water fountain or bring a bottled water).

d. Allow students to splash water on their faces when they use the bathroom.

4. Design

Individuals diagnosed with the Hyperactive-Impulsive type of ADHD are full of energy and are often "on the go" running and bumping into things or touching people. They may be clumsy and hurt themselves or knock things down. Design is related to how a classroom is arranged. To accommodate these individuals they would need an informal design.

a. Provide a safe environment and tools which would prevent them from running into peers or desks (or into the street after a ball).

b. Use a variety of desks or seating choices such as hard desks, cushions, sofas, carpet, or carrels. In other words, provide an informal design in the classroom which is one that would accommodates all students.

c. Seat students near the teacher's desk and other appropriate places.

27

d. Use tables for limited group work, horseshoe arrangement for larger group discussions, and rows of desks for individual work.

e. Provide comfortable lighting and room temperatures.

f. Give other students in the class alternative interpretations of being touched by a child with ADHD (i.e., the touching is not necessarily hitting or fighting rather one way of being friendly or being frustated).

Emotional Stimuli (Motivation, persistence, responsibility, and structure)

1. Motivation

Individuals with ADHD become bored easily and are restless. They are often described as lazy.

a. Increase the pace of lesson presentations (i.e., use a slower pace).

b. Provide a variety of activities for each lesson to prevent boredom or to enhance interest.

c. Use multi-sensory presentations (pictures, sound, tactual, and visual materials). Make sure the materials are related directly to the learning content. Example: jumping rope can be an educational exercise if incorporated into the content of the learner.

d. Make lessons brief. If a student can demonstrate that she knows how to solve similar problems, why give her a sheet with 25 or 30 to do?

e. Use distributed practice rather than mass practice (i.e., break presentations or assignments into small segments).

f. Allow students to take frequent breaks with the understanding that they must return to the task often until it is completed.

g. Permit the student to be involved as a teacher's aide to keep the student alert.

h. Make lessons entertaining and enjoyable. The teacher and the student can be actors. Use psychodrama.

i. Vary the instructional medium (visual and auditory materials; and tactual/kinesthetic activities.

j. Allow students to make choices and to select tasks and activities that are interesting to them as long as it is related to the topic.

k. Give students a choice to perform a task the way he prefers as long as they learn or achieve the objective of the assignment. Alternative ways of solving problems are effective for any student.

l. Set several deadlines to allow a student to either select the one she prefers or an opportunity to submit assignments, in part, at each deadline point. This strategy teaches them to plan for the future.

2. Persistence

Individuals with ADHD exhibit low levels of endurance; they give up easily on tasks. Some individuals become hyperfocuced and remain on tasks too long.

a. Allow students who give up quickly to take frequent breaks but to understand that he must return to a task until it is completed.

b. Give short quizzes and avoid long tests or give tests piecemeal.

c. Avoid timed tests when possible. In other words, allow the student to complete her work. She may know the answer but did not have time to complete it. Also, give the student time to check their work after its completion.

d. Allow students to use timers, watches or stop clocks to begin and end tasks. This strategy can help the person who is hyperfocused to stop or complete the work within a certain duration of time.

e. Ask students with ADHD to estimate how long it would take to do a task. This strategy will give the student an exercise in planning.

f. Allow the student to set his own time and race against the time, if he is slow or hyperfocused. Parents could give their child exercises in racing against the clock (make it a game while they are learning).

3. Responsibility (Conforming)

The individual who is diagnosed with ADHD appears to be irresponsible; has to be reminded, monitored, and constantly reinforced; and are often late or absent.

a. Offer choices and alternatives.

b. Consider student-designed tasks and study assignments for those who want or need responsibility.

    c. Assign short-term assignments.

    d. Praise individuals for making decisions themselves.

    e. Teach students how to check or monitor tasks. Do not bring attention to the child when monitoring or checking them.

    f. Allow individuals to check their own work before you do; reinforce the same.

    g. Choose/provide variety an interesting tasks and tasks to match the students' interests.

    h. Apply the "self-fulfilling prophecy" (i.e., teach students to make positive affirmations and positive statements.

    i. Stand, walk nearby or seat the student near your desk to be able to cue him or her as necessary.

    j. Teach students how to use watches, clocks, and timers (e.g., set a watch or clock about 15 minutes fast and pretend that is the correct time; or set a timer to gauge the duration of time spent on a task).

4. Structure

The individual with ADHD learns or works more productively in environments of low structure; they are low on "order" (appear "messy" and disorganized). Realize that the individual may have an internal sense of organization.

    a. Allow students to make use of tools such as watches, timers, folders and dividers.

    b. Devote time for all students to organize their notebooks, desks, and lockers.

    c. Provide for free expression, psychodrama or role play in learning activities.

    d. Provide for variety in every sense imaginable (most students will benefit, not just those with ADHD).

Sociological Stimuli (Self, pair, peers, team, adult, varied)

1. Colleague

The self-esteem of individuals with ADHD appears to be affected and they feel that they are stupid, lazy or unmotivated. Students report that peers and adults respond to them in ways that make them feel odd. Teachers and classroom managers can produce a classroom atmosphere where students can feel good about themselves.

    a. Recognize students by using his/her name in your presentations.

    b. Write personal notes to the student about key elements in the lesson.

    c. Teach and treat high school and college levels collegially.

    d. Treat younger students older than they are.

2. Self

Typically, the individual with ADHD is people-oriented and want to study/work with others either in pairs or groups; they often find it difficult to work alone; they love to talk and socialize and often are penalized for doing so.

    a. Arrange adequate space between desks wide enough so that students cannot touch each other or place carrels in class for students to use.

    b. Use horseshoe arrangement when independent work and group discussion are required.

    c. Use a table and assign 3-4 in a group when group work is required.

    d. Use carrels or use booths for tests and other individual seat work.

    e. Allow ADHD student to work alone, if preferred or necessary.

3. Pair

    a. Use peer tutoring when possible to help review concepts.

    b. Allow the students to tutor others, especially younger children.

    c. Give the student the choice to work with another peer, if peer-oriented.

4. Team

    a. Use cooperative learning activities.

    b. Permit the student to share the part of the information they contributed on a team. Insure that they have made a contribution.

   c. Allow students to help others in small groups.

   d. Use team learning, circle of knowledge, and other group activities and approaches.

5. Authority

Some ADHD students will perform better for a parent, teachers, or other special persons in their lives.

   a. Get these special persons involved with working with the student at home.

   b. Request these special persons to visit the classroom and help as a teacher's aide.

   c. Allow students to be in his favorite teacher's room, if possible or to be supervised by special people.

   d. Match students with certain teachers, when possible.

6. Varied

Some ADHD students become bored easily; most prefer variety.

   a. Provide a variety of learning activities and experiences.

   b. Use multi-sensory materials.

   c. Use multiple approaches to teaching.

   d. Give instructions or directions or make statements in different ways.

   e. Begin new or difficult learning materials in the student's strongest modality and rotate them through the other modalities.

   f. Go "heavy" with tactual/kinesthetic activities.

Physical Stimuli (Perceptual, intake, time, and mobility)

1. Perceptual Modalities

Visual, auditory, tactual, and kinesthetic are the four perceptual modalities. Be modality specific with new and difficult content. The individual who is diagnosed with ADHD is highly mobile and tactual; they are not effective listeners and do not like visual tasks such as reading.

 a. Use hands-on manipulatives and activities in teaching the subject.

 b. Use game-like activities to teach various content.

 c. Use floor games whenever possible to teach math and other content.

 d. Use A-V aids, audio tapes, videos, and the TV when suggested.

 e. Use multi-sensory resources.

 f. Allow students with ADHD to demonstrate and share information.

 g. Use *in vivo* experiences (i.e., real objects and experiences in real life).

 h. Incorporate field trips as a learning approach.

 i. Capitalize on the person's need to move and be active by designing learning activities which require the person to move and touch.

 j. Use drama to illustrate and allow student to act and role play.

2. Intake

The individual with ADHD is energetic and "on the go;" therefore, their metabolic rate is high. Those who are on behavioral stimulants may have loss of appetite. Parents usually report that their child with ADHD usually has a good appetite.

 a. Provide the opportunity for individuals to snack and drink, if desired while studying.

 b. Allow individuals to eat/drink while taking tests.

 c. Allow the individual's parents to provide the snacks.

 d. Allow students to snack during the frequent breaks.

3. Time of Day

Individuals or parents of students with ADHD invariably report that they stay up late at night and sleep late in the mornings; their energy level is low during the early part of the day.

   a. Schedule the most demanding tasks in the afternoons and evenings if she begins to lose focus during the day.

   b. Arrange an activity around the student's learning style.

   c. Omit naps at school especially if the student resists a nap at school.

4. Mobility

An individual diagnosed with ADHD is restless, fidgety, squirms in seat, or leaves his seat. An alternative description or interpretation is that the individual is a kinesthetic learner or has a strong need to move about.

   a. Provide role playing activities to act out key concepts and content.

   b. Use floor games to teach math, reading and to do tests.

   c. Capitalize on the tendency to move by assigning tasks that require movement.

   d. Use drama to teach some ideas.

   e. Design learning activities where students can use their bodies such as dance, pantomime, or charades.

Psychological (Global, analytic, hemisphericity, impulsivity vs. reflective)

1. Analytic vs. Global

The ADHD student is more global than analytic, will have several things going on at once, and may not remember to complete them.

   a. Require the use of a watch, a timer, a scheduler, dividers for the desk and notebook, lists of what is inside on the cover and dividers for books or by subject.

   b. Require the child to set his/her watch 5-10 minutes ahead of time to prevent being late

   c. Require the child to use a timer and race with the timer going off in completing tasks. Practice often until the time shortens and a habit is formed.

   d. Train students to use watch or timer to give him/her a signal to stop working on task A and go on to task

   e. Train students to place things where they belong immediately

f. Train the student to have a certain place for everything.

g. Train the student how to organize on the computer

h. Train the student to call and leave messages on his home phone things he needs to do.

i. Train students to make "TO DO" lists daily and tape on refrigerator, desk, or note book.

2. Cerebral Preference

An individual with ADHD thinks divergently which causes her to be disorganized; is a perfectionist (a trait of giftedness, which works against productivity and rate of productivity; or procrastinates. She processes information primarily from the right side of the brain; and processes information simultaneously rather than successively. ADHD students learn like the typical global student.

a. Use story context to assist students in figuring out unknown content.

b. Teach through stories and use examples that are interesting or relevant to the student.

c. Use analogies, parables, comic strips, and humor in teaching information.

d. Permit the use of fantasy and allow students to use humor, cartoon, dance, and music.

e. Emphasize the study of graphics (tables, pictures, and inserts).

3. Reflective vs. Impulsive

Students with ADHD are impulsive, they speak and act without thinking; or want to be the first one to finish work. They blurt out answers or complete sentences before others can ask the question or finish their statement.

a. Collect students' work individually as finished to reduce time pressure or urge to be first.

b. Ask the student to think of more than one way to do a task before doing it.

c. Train students to say "let me think about it" before he speaks, quote an answer, or act.

d. Make sure students understand what you say before s/he does a task by requiring eye contact when given directions/instructions

e. Require students to repeat or paraphrase what you have said to them before beginning a task.

These are the populations of behaviors that can be shown by children, adolescents (and even adults) with ADHD). No individual presents with all of them; only a subset. Work with the subset of behaviors your child or student presents. Problems can be alleviated and coping skills can be acquired when the appropriate intervention is matched to a specific set of symptoms or behaviors.

Summary

The book describes a multimodal approach to addressing Attention Deficit Hyperactivity Disorder with an emphasis on psychological/behavioral, and educational/learning style approaches. Content includes etiological theories, both medical and non-drug approaches, the DSM-IV-TR criteria, and interventions to treat the core conditions, as well as, executive functions and problems of organization, memory, and social interactions.

Emphasis is placed on addressing executive functions first and early as symptoms of ADHD are observed in very young children. Parents will know how to detect the conditions as early as infancy; teachers will know how to teach students with the disorder; and mental health professionals can integrate the information in the treatment of the individual and the family. The latter part of the book is more of a guide to working with individuals with the disorder whether a person is on prescribed medications or not.

Throughout the book, the point is made that parents, teachers, and mental health providers (medical or non-medical) need training in Attention Deficit Hyperactivity Disorder due to its prevalence worldwide. Evidence-based research on the treatment is in the literature ranging from individual studies to the Multimodal Treatment Study of ADHD by the National Institute of Mental Health. It needs to be "pulled together" and shared in terms that are workable and easy to apply by parents, teachers, and mental health professionals. Effectiveness is the result of working together.

Some ADHD Resources

I.   National Institutes of Mental Health (NIMH), (304) 443-4513.
II.   Centers for Disease Control and Prevention (CDCP), (800) 232-4636.
III.   CHADD - A national resource center on ADHD, (800) 238-4050.
IV.   Resources by State and Municipality:
        A. State Department of Education, Special Education Services
        B. Advocacy Groups
        C. Support Groups
V.   References (Page 33)

REFERENCES

American Academy of Pediatrics, Clinical Practice Guideline: Treatment of the School-Aged Child with Attention Deficit Hyperactivity Disorder. *Pediatrics. 108.* (2001). 1033-1034.

American Psychiatric Association. (2000). *Diagnostic and Statistical Manual of Mental Disorders-IV-TR.* APA Press, Washington, DC.

American Psychiatric Association. (2000). Attention-deficit/hyperactivity disorder. In: *Diagnostic and Statistical Manual of Mental Disorders DSM-IV-TR.* 4th ed. Arlington, VA.

Anderson, V., Jacobs, R. & Anderson, P. (2008). Executive functions and the frontal lobes: A lifespan perspective. New York: Psychology Press.

Andries, D. (2006). Increasing memory in ADHD students: Lecture strategies helpful when dealing with students with ADHD or ADD. http://addadhd-suite101.com.

Austin, M., Reiss, N., & Burgdorf, L. (2007). Learning Disorder Early Speech Communication problems. Centersite.net.

Barbaressi, W. (2007). *Archives of Pediatrics and Adolescent Medicine.* 21.Barbaressi, W., et al. (2007). How many people have ADHD? *Attitude Magazine.*

Barkley, R. A. Murphy, K & Kwasnik, D. (1996). Psychological adjustment and adaptive impairments in young adults with ADHD. *Journal of Attention Deficit Disorder, 1, 130-131.*

Barkley, R. A. (1995). Taking charge of ADHD. New York: Guilford Press.

Barkley, R.A. (2005). Take charge of ADHD: The complete authoritative guide for parents. New York: Guilford Publications.

Biederman, J. & Faraone, S. (2004). The Massachusetts General Hospital studies of gender influences on ADHD in youth and relatives. *Psychiatric Clinical North America, 27,* 225-232.

Boller, Barbara. (2008). Teaching organizational skills in middle school: Moving toward independence. ERIC, 81, 169-171.

Bor, W., Sanders, M. & Markie-Dadds, C. (2002). The effects of the triple-positive parenting program on preschool children with co-occurring disruptive behavior and attentional/hyperactivity difficulties. *Journal of Abnormal Child Psychology, 30,* 571-586.

Brown, T. (2007). A new approach to Attention Deficit Hyperactivity Disorder. Educational   Leadership, 22-27.

Brown, T. (2003). ADHD as executive function Impairments *(reprinted from the Summer/Fall issue of The Help Group's HelpLetter.* ADHD as Executive Function Impairments.

Bussing, R., Schoenberg, N. E. & Perwien, A. R.- (1998). Knowledge and information about ADHD: Evidence of cultural differences among African-American and white parents. *Social Science and Medicine, 46,* 919-933.

Castellanos, F. & Rapoport, J. (1992). Etiology of attention deficit hyperactivity disorder. *Child and Adolescent Psychiatry Clinical North America, 1,* 373-384.

Center for Learning Disabilities. (2009). CPS Psychosocial Paediatrics Committee. (2003). Canadian Paediatric Society.

Chandler, J. (2002). *Pamphlet Series.*

Conrad, P. (2006). Identifying hyperactive children. New York: Ashgate.

Dendy, C. A. Z. (2002). *Attention Magazine.* 5 components of executive function and A bird's eye view of life with ADD and ADHD: Advice from Young Survivors.

Dunn, R., & Dunn, K. (1972). *Practical Approaches to Individualizing Instruction: Contracts and Other Effective Teaching Strategies.* Nyack, NY: Parker Publishing Company, a Prentice Hall Division.

Dunn, R., & Dunn, K. & Price, G.E. (1975, 1979, 1985, 1987, 1989). *Learning Style* Inventory. Lawrence, KS: Price Systems, Inc.

Dunn, R., Dunn, K. & Price, G.E., (1979, 1982, 1991). *Productivity Environmental Preference Survey.* Lawrence, KS: Price Systems, Inc.

Encyclopedia of Mental Health. (2009).

Faraone S. V. (2003). Understanding the Effect Size of ADHD Medications: Implications for Clinical Care. Medscape Psychiatry & Mental Health (ADHD Expert Column Series).

FDA Directs ADHD Drug Manufacturers to Notify Patients about Cardiovascular Adverse Events and Psychiatric Adverse Events. (2007). *FDA News.* Media Inquiries: Sandy Walsh, 301-827.

FDA Guideline: Attention-deficit hyperactivity disorder. (2005). University of Michigan Health System. Attention-deficit hyperactivity disorder.

Fine, L. (2002). Study: Minimum ADHD Incidence is 7.5 Percent. *Education Week.*

Gershon, J. & Gershan, J. (2002). A meta-analytic review of gender differences in ADHD. *Journal of Attention Disorders, 5, 143-154.*

Goldberg, D. (2004). School organization tips for students with ADHD and Learning Disabilities. *ADDitude Magazine.*

Goodman, R. & Stevenson, J. (1989). A twin study of hyperactivity, II: The etiological role of genes, family relationships and perinatal adversity. *Journal of Child Psychological Psychiatry,* 691-709.

Goldstein, S. 91996). Attention deficit hyperactivity in children: Current issues. *The Medical Psychotherapist,* 12

Havey, J. M. Olson, J. M.; McCormick, C. & Cates, G. L. (2005). Teachers' Perceptions of the Incidence and Management of Attention-Deficit Hyperactivity Disorder. *Applied Neuropsychology,* 7 (2), 120-127.

Health News Digest.com (2005, August 29). Why many girls with ADHD are often overlooked. Retrieved August 29, 2005, from the *American Psychological Association* Website: http://www.psycport.com.

Hechtman, L., Hinshaw, S. P., Pelham, W. E., & Swanson, J. M. (1995). NIMH collaborative multisite multimodal treatment study of children with ADHD: I. Background and rationale. *Journal of the American Academy of Child and Adolescent Psychiatry, 34*(8), 987–1000.

Hoza, B.. (2006). Peer Functioning in Children With ADHD

Hynd, G., Hem, K., Voeller, K. & Marshall, R. (1991). Neurologocal basis of attention deficit disorder. *School*

Psychology Review, 20, 174-178.

Iannelli, V. (2008). ADHD Treatment Guidelines New Treatment Recommendations for Children with ADHD. *About.com Health's Disease and Condition Content.*

Ianelli, V. (2005). Straterra--A new medication. about.com newsletter.

Irlen, H. (1983). Successful treatment of learning disabilities. Paper presented at the 91st Annual Convention of the the the APA, Anaheim, CA.

Ingersoll, B. (1988). *Your Hyperactive Child: A Parent's Guide to Coping with Attention Deficit Disorder.* New York: Doubleday.

Lesaca, T. (2001). Executive functions in parents with ADHD. *Psychiatric Times,* 18 (11), 1.

Magyary, D. & Brandt, P. (2002). A decision tree and clinical paths for the assessment and management of children with ADHD. *Issues in Mental Health Nursing,* 23, 553 – 566.

Maidment, I. D. (2003). The use of antidepressants to treat Attention deficit hyperactivity disorder. *Journal of Psychopharmacology,* 17(3), 332-336.

Martin, B. (2007). an article/brochure, *Resources for ADHD,* published by the National Institute of Mental Health.

Meltzer, L. (2007). *Executive Function in Education: From Theory to Practice,* (editor). Guildford Press.

Mayo Clinic Staff. (2009). Attention-deficit/hyperactivity disorder (ADHD) in children. MayoClinic.com.

McCormick, C. & Cates, G. L. (2005). Teachers' Perceptions of the Incidence and Management of Attention-Deficit Hyperactivity Disorder. *Applied Neuropsychology,* 7 (2), 120-127.

Meltzer, D. & Kalyani K. in *Executive Function in Education: From Theory to Practice.* http://www.cec.sped.org, 2007.

Meyer, R. (2007). Psychological Treatment for children with ADHD (white paper). http://www.childdevelopmentinfo.com/ADHD/add-evidence-basedtrt.htm.

Moffitt, T. & Melchior, M. (2007). Why does the worldwide prevalence of childhood attention deficit hyperactivity disorder matter? *American Journal of Psychiatry,* 164, 856.

National Center for Learning Disabilities. (2009). Executive functioning fact sheet. http://www.ncld.org/content/view/865/391/.

National Institutes of Mental Health. (2006 rev).NIH Publication No. 3572.

National Institutes of Mental Health Internet Report. (1996). Attention Deficit Hyperactivity Disorder: Decade of the brain. http://www.nimh.nih.gov/publicat/adhd.htm.

National Institutes of Mental Health (1999). ADHD, a 14-month randomized clinical trial treatment strategies for ADHD. The MRTA Cooperative Group, Multimodal treatment study of children with ADHD. *Archives of General Psychiatry* 56-96.

NINDS Attention Deficit-Hyperactivity Disorder Information Page. National Institute of Neurological Disorders and Stroke (NINDS/NIH) February 9, 2007.

O'Reily, S. (2007). Teaching students with ADHD. Unpublished Master's thesis, The Evergreen State College, Olympia, WA.

Pastor, P. N. (2005). *Public Health Report.* 120(4), 383-392.

Pelham Jr., W.E., & Hoza, B. (2002). Responsiveness in interaction of mothers and sons with ADHD: Relations to maternal and child characteristics. *Journal of Abnormal Child Psychology,* 30 (1), 77 – 88.

Polanczyk, G. & Rohde, L. (2007). *American Journal of Psychiatry, 164, 1612-1613 (Letter to the Editor).*

Powell, K. Voeller, K. (2004). Prefrontal executive function syndromes in children. *Journal Child Neurology,* 19, 785-797.

Quinn, C. Wilens, T., Spencer, T. and the Harris ADHD Working Group. (2004). Perception of girls and ADHD. *Medscape General Medicine.* 2; 6 (2):

Samuel, V. J. Curtis, S. A. Thornell, A., George, P., Taylor, A. D. Brome, R., & Biederman, J. (1997) The unexplored void of ADHD and African-American research: A review of the literature. *Journal of Attention Disorder.* 7 (1), 197-207.

Spencer, T., Biedmerman, J., Wilens, T. Steingard, R. Geist, D. (2007). Nortriptyline Treatment of Children with Attention-deficit Hyperactivity Disorder and Tic Disorder or Tourette's Syndrome. *Journal of the American Academy of Child & Adolescent Psychiatry.*

Timothy Lesaca. (2001). Psychiatric Times,18 (11).

Vereb, R. & DiPerna, J. (2004). Teacher's knowledge of ADHD, treatments for ADHD, and treatment acceptability: An initial investigation. *School Psychology Review,* 33, 421-428.

Zametkin, A. J. (1995). Attention-deficit Disorder: Born to be Hyperactive? *Journal of the American Medical Association,* 273, 1871-1874

Zentall, A.. (1983). Learning environments: A review of physical and temporal factors. *Exceptional Education Quarterly,* 4, 90-115.

Waxmonsky, J. G. (2005). Nonstimulant therapies for attention-deficit hyperactivity disorder (ADHD) in children and adults. *Essential Psychopharmacology.* 6(5), 262-276.

Williams, L., Swanson, J, & Wigal, T. (1995). Minority assessment of ADHD: Issues in the development of new assessment techniques. *Attention!*

Zamba, D. (2008). Identifying girls with the inattentive type. *Intervention in School and Clinic, 44,* 34-40.

Images:
Images used are from the Broderbund ClickArt 1,200,000 series, (c) 2002-2006 Riverdeep Interactive Learning Limited, and its licensors.

Cover, Layout and Design: Jerome Saintjones

SUBJECT INDEX

www.ingramcontent.com/pod-product-compliance
Lightning Source LLC
Chambersburg PA
CBHW060506060326
40689CB00020B/4653